AF171193

Books of Theo von Taane

book	ISBN / order nr.
Football Tacticboard & Training Workbook	9783734749605
Badminton Tacticboard & Training Workbook	9783734749643
Baseball Tacticboard & Training Workbook	9783734749650
Basketball Tacticboard & Training Workbook	9783734749681
Bowling Tacticboard & Training Workbook	9783734749698
Cricket Tacticboard & Training Workbook	9783734749711
Ice Hockey Tacticboard & Training Workbook	9783734749728
Fencing Tacticboard & Training Workbook	9783734749735
Field Hockey Tacticboard & Training Workbook	9783734749810
Football (Soccer) Tacticboard & Training Workbook	9783734749827
Futsal Tacticboard & Training Workbook	9783734749834
Handball Tacticboard & Training Workbook	9783734749841
Lacrosse Women Tacticboard & Training Workbook	9783734749858
Lacrosse Men Tacticboard & Training Workbook	9783734749865
Netball Tacticboard & Training Workbook	9783734749872
Rugby Tacticboard & Training Workbook	9783734749889
Chess Tacticboard & Training Workbook	9783734749896
Squash Tacticboard & Training Workbook	9783734749902
Tennis Tacticboard & Training Workbook	9783734749919
Table Tennis Tacticboard & Training Workbook	9783734749926
Volleyball Tacticboard & Training Workbook	9783739232775
Water Polo Tacticboard & Training Workbook	9783734749940

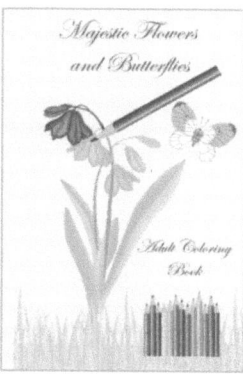

Majestic Flowers and Butterflies
- Adult Coloring Book - ISBN: 9783739227085

This coloring book for adults contains 36 beautiful patterns of various flowers. Experience hours full of stress relief, mindful calm, creative expression and fun.
Use crayons, felt-tip pens and colored pencils to give the patterns a personal touch.
Millions of people worldwide have rediscovered the simple relaxation and joy of coloring!
Join this community and find yourself enchanted by the magical passion of inspiring coloring.

Theo von Taane

Water Polo 2 in 1 Tacticboard & Training Workbook

The 2 in 1 Tacticboard & Training Workbook for fast creation of coaching instructions/game tactics and schemes, doesn't only offer sport specific preprints (playing field and space for notes), but also a cover, usable as a dry erase panel (whiteboard pen is needed).

ADVANTAGES:

- notebook with sport specific preprints (playing field) for fast and simple sketching of coaching instructions/game tactics and schemes

- If all pages of the notebook are used, the cover is still a dry erase panel (tacticboard)

- Due to a handy format, the notebook can be comfortably used in any situation (e.g. on the way or on the playing field)

- Perfect for spontaneous collection of ideas or as a memorization tool

- Practical handling due to easy pocket format

Bibliografische Information der Deutschen Nationalbibliothek:
Die Deutsche Nationalbibliothek verzeichnet diese Publikation in der Deutschen Nationalbibliografie; detaillierte bibliografische Daten sind im Internet über http://dnb.dnb.de abrufbar.

© 2016 Theo von Taane; 2. Auflage

Texte und Illustrationen: **Theo von Taane**

Herstellung und Verlag: BoD – Books on Demand, Norderstedt

ISBN: 9783734749940